LITTLE NEST

Wick Poetry Chapbook Series Five
Catherine Wing, Editor

Poppy Seeds
Allison Davis

Here Both Sweeter
Daniel Carter

I Left My Wings on a Chair
Karen Schubert

Determinant
Alex Fabrizio

Local Fauna
Brian Brodeur

Little Nest
Diana Lueptow

LITTLE NEST

Poems by Diana Lueptow

The Kent State University Press
Kent, Ohio

Ohio Arts Council
A STATE AGENCY
THAT SUPPORTS PUBLIC
PROGRAMS IN THE ARTS

ISBN 978-1-60635-249-6
Manufactured in the United States of America

The Wick Poetry Series is sponsored in part by the Wick Poetry Center at Kent State University.

Cataloging information for this title is available at the Library of Congress.

CONTENTS

ACKNOWLEDGMENTS

I am grateful to editors of the following journals for these previous publications:

Arion: "Demeter," "For Elizabeth," "Rodin's *Fallen Caryatid Carrying Her Stone,*" "Theseus Hears the Voice of Ariadne"; *Beloit Poetry Journal:* "Little Eucharistic Song," "Possum Idyll"; *FIELD:* "Ariadne at Sugarloaf Key"; *Plainsongs:* "Five Mourning Doves"; *RHINO:* "Peripherally Yours"; *The Stinging Fly:* "Sense Memory Cares for Us Like a Mother."

Thank you to my family and friends, and to my mentors, for guidance and inspiration in the making of these poems.

LITTLE EUCHARISTIC SONG

O chrysanthemum, you are so evolved,
so selected to live communally.
What fine scale. Yes, we could learn from that.

But if we had to act as *one* flower
yet be in fact two hundred, it would go
so hard on us. Your petals, worlds. Your worlds

are cups to suck the windy water.
The new thing is inside. Sheaf of pistils—
Oh, oh. That *is* too much. Oh no. Oh you.

THESEUS HEARS THE VOICE OF ARIADNE

Thinks, it worked. Stupid string of golden thread!
Worked, yes, and someone holds the other end.
Whereas, the dream I have from time to time—

the one where you come back from the dead
but keep avoiding me—may signify . . .
what? Neither of us thinks I helped you much,

I guess, or it's none of my business what
the afterlife is like, or isn't it
enough, now, this self-indulgent dreamland

of complaint? Time to wind it up. We are
not gods, not heroes. Not Theseus,
that fucker, arms wide, who sprints to safety.

See him as he understands. Nearly
blooming—the wonder and relief flush
on his face, eyes bright in the foul passage.

About that face. Call that a look of love?

RODIN'S *FALLEN CARYATID CARRYING HER STONE*

The idea is that she tumbled down,
is it, with construction under way?
Or could not do her part. Or maybe

the other girls kicked her out. Anyway
she's here now, doubled on one haunch,
ready to shove this monster off, or ready

to love it to pieces, chunk of bronze
like her. She's not so bad a fit—but she's

never been happy in a crouch, never,
to be honest, though she's stuck with it—
the cold museum, glass gallery,

hushed museum at night.

STARGAZER

Anatolia, 3000 B.C.

She is the sadness of having been somewhere before.
Windswept, pine scrubbed, singed. Of slingshot galaxies

she was an ovoid watcher, stretched sky.
Mere dots for eyes, suggestions barely raised.

She is substance supported by a narrow stem.
Not fritillaries or lilies of the valley,

a necessary poise precludes such nodding
sisterhoods. Her purposes are hidden. Staying

power. She is austere, small, smooth in hand,
one imagines, once. She is magnificent, rough

from lying roughly. Who left her in the earth,
abandoned, sacrificed, offered, deposited, sown?

She is the indecision of open thought, or
the steadiness of belief. The breath she takes

has never been exhaled, the soft lips—how can marble
do that?—and faint, angled profile wait for us.

The corridor of her display becomes a temple.
You might say she is hope, being so attentive.

FOR ELIZABETH

after Sappho

Kore: shadow play. Behind the drape,
in the dressing room you were busy.
Backlit, the slow arch of your arm—

you were twelve—grew big in silhouette.

*And there, when they had stirred
the magic liquor in the jug—*

Where I waited in the hallway, there I watched
you turn a woman. Gestures large, moving
on the drape like clouds on a rippling sea.

*and Hermes, in each held out cup
had poured from a leather bottle
every god his ambrosia—*

*each tipped some out, for piety,
and rang his cup against another,
that all bright and noble things*

woman in play, and shadow—

come to our new kinsman.

DEMETER

Wayne County, Ohio

Already I've lost you, you there thinking
that here it comes, the substitution
of metaphor and myth for real, lived life.

But how do you know? You are not here
in deepening night on this unlighted road
between two cornfields. You don't see

how the stalks lash about, how the wind
stirs these dark acres, how many thousands
of lightning bugs ascend. This is alone—

the wish to sleep by the side of the road,

one view lunar halo, the other storm clouds
rolling flashes in the cup. Contours—
tree, barn, farm—bleed out.

                          The world was in turmoil.
There was too much sun. There was too much rain.

But do you see how someone might return?

THE FUNERAL OF TOUCH

I've made the calls that had to be made. I've called
the skin of my wrist to let it know, and called
the cord of my shoulders once loosened by your thumbs.

The rites for what comes next are Byzantine.
They're partly hidden. The cantor and priest sing
parastas, the wake for the body, hollows

under knees, absence of fingertips on cold glass.
At the holy mass the book is held high: *written
indeed* the priest says, and *vos kress,* what is risen;

wisdom! attend! he says, word woven brazenly
into the body's farewell.
                            The Husband's Message,
old Saxon poem, made its very body greet

the wife and its first words courted her
the courtesy of telling its own life. *Now
I will tell thee apart my lineage as a tree.*

As if the matter of salutation stood in
for an actual hail. As if that lord's letter
might contain the waiting man for the wife who held it.

As if the greeting could stand in for the person.
As if this poem could stand for you.
                            In the story,
he'd escaped with his life in a wooden boat.

Rough hull. Crash and splash. Scratch of halyard.
How to speak of it, the forgetting. I wonder whom
to tell, or if one good-bye is enough for everyone.

INANIMATE

When he was small the man was told
by a teacher that he hurt the pencil
when he chewed it. Strange, horror

inflicted on a child to make him good.
Ever after, he tended carefully to objects, tools,
helpless things. Iron skillets scoured with salt,

a brightening swipe of oil on garden shears.
His duties were clear. Now what
is he supposed to do with people, who

can help themselves but don't? Not clear.
The man had heard that Darwin said
the suffering of the smaller animals

throughout endless time was more
than he could bear to think of. The man

admired that pain, made from mercy.

EQUATORIAL

We'd crossed it as we slept,
and dreamt of penguins drifting north.

Those penguins knew they had gone far enough.
Or come too far. Funny what we do not know,

as if we'd earned this brooding calm.
I mean us. In our dreams, in our days

—on the waves a nest is floating—

watery and measured.

LAUREL SLICK

Could be woman or plant, mountain or man.
How to tell mountain laurel from rhododendron
is: short leaf, short name; long leaf, long name.
Once laurel was *ivy,* and rhodie was *laurel.*
Shorter yet. I'll tell you, I can't say
the difference is obvious. A slick is
both together. Rounding a trail in the Blue Ridge
I turned into something else, as sometimes laurel
is lambkill. I turned into thinking and not thinking.
I came into an airy cove, high in the side
of Mount Pisgah, where I was half embraced
by rightward branches—trail gone, all still—
and leftward fell across my neck long-fingered
leaves, and before me in the circlet's gap
were far-off mountains, drifting mist, hawk
sailing the interim. A tiny danger
as the boat turns in to the wind, stalling
to change direction. There was no breath anymore
for one man. There was breath upon another's
cheek from the other man. Petrarch
was a mountaineer. He climbed Mont Ventoux,
saw a wreath of clouds, Italy, the Rhone, the sea.
I see what the imagination is.
I was given a hiking stick of laurel
from the mountains. Or, rhododendron.
Most likely, the archaic coronet was
oak leaves. Amongst the highland laurels Wright
made a jutting house as if of those ledges
common where I'm from. As a people,
we couldn't see to it now, I don't think—
the parkway of the Blue Ridge.

MINK AND RABBIT

Nimble isn't the half of it. Fierce is, mink
is, bounding. Rabbit is, panting. Mine—
sighting down path through riparian thicket.

Let's step back. Meadows cut by a
mown path, sweet in late afternoon. Rabbit
dashing across the path. Elegance

of pure form. Brushstroke black after it.
Here am I, aglow in afternoon sun
with admiration. The jumping

with awareness. Second dash of rabbit.
Brushstroke bound to bound there, after it.
After it. The leaps becoming all of it.

Let me stop right there. Go nimbly back to
the before-awareness part. The sureness
of those leaps, those bounds.

SIX MOURNING DOVES

Here's the deal. One story, plus another
leaving something I guess to be desired.
A story from my grandfather, whose mother,
on the Wisconsin homestead he recalled,
once fell ill—no cause, so no one had a cure.
But at last the doctor told her that her need
was for a dish of mourning doves, six birds
exactly. So her sons went out and shot
six doves, made soup, or whatever mourning
is made into, and *My land, if that didn't work.*
Sick of nothing and well of six gray doves.
Upon that conclusion, my grandfather
savored his story, hated the other.
His father all summer farmed him out.

A WINTERTIME DREAM OF BEES

We are the ghosts of bees you gassed last summer.

Our swarm had busied itself between door frame
and brick—flotillas in, flotillas out—
a crack too comfy for our own good.

Before long, doom. Scène pathétique. Next day

the foragers and scouts came drifting back. Now
we linger in soffits and eaves, little wisps
of your regret (you could have called a bee man)

and though it was night we did not die asleep
as you had hoped (your kind of planning)
and as for rest, your doubts are what you

burrow in at night, aren't they? Little nest.
But your hopes and doubts—
                      they're not our concern.

IN MOSER'S TENDER WOOD ENGRAVING

In Moser's tender wood engraving, Dove,
the dove in profile stares from its left eye,
whose black disk of a pupil is circled
in pale gray, ringed by another circle
of black, dotted by a highlight of reflection,
a particle of something within the eyesight
of the dove, eyesight guarded by little feathers
edging the eye's socket, minute crosshatches
smaller than the still small feathers in ruffles
down the neck, or the shallow tuft of feathers
at the ridge of the sharp nib of the beak
in Moser's tender wood engraving, Dove.

SWEET SEA

Said Champlain, delighted. Inland oceans,
thick with fish and solid underfoot
in winter. *Felicitations,* the beeches

whisper. Misery Bay to Graveyard Pond—

Perry's men, not battle-ready or sea-legged,
after beating Earth's great navy,

two ships, two brigs two schooners & one sloop.

Perry must have thought, everything to the bold.

They tramped across, over Presque Isle Bay, for food.

SENSE MEMORY CARES FOR US LIKE A MOTHER

My friend said the skate, flayed, waiting
for the pan, its flesh had stung him;
arm trembling, he slid the fish into the oil
which soon made sweet the flesh,
made soft the bitter Amarone wine,
the bitter greens. Still stinging, he said
while I ate; I ate while mind
slid out the ray-like skate, slid in
a puppyish ray that surfaced in its tank
at the aquarium—nodding up, and up
for my pat on its soft head: touch, a touch,
yes that is all, a tap a tap, on living skin.
That's how it is, you see, memory embracing
us as a mother would, trying to make right.

PERIPHERALLY YOURS

Supposedly for snakes, our vision snakes
down sideways as if drawn there. To guard,
say scientists who study antecedents.

That's us, the learning ones, who learned
our animal gestures early. Before we spoke
we told each other things. Later we taught

words slowly to our bodies, which already

knew to shy away, to turn toward, to reach.
For instance. His glance at me, his turn, oh

toward me—I saw them—quick as that.

COMPLAINT TO EROS

Are you responsible for this? People
whose fantasy it is to lose their limbs.

Beyond fantastic. They think, they plan, they

find physicians. Who will chop—something,
to start: one arm, one leg. On the theory,

perhaps, the presumption of keeping something

whole inside. Do you craft everyone's desire?

A woman, swimming lone and nude at night,
hauls herself to the pool's rim, phones her lover.

Are you he, not altogether there?

HYMN

Bluebirds chase each other into the briars
and out, rustle and thrash of their wings
in the brambles contained and then released

raucously in courtship. White breasts of swallows
take fire from sunset, scarab heads dipping across
the meadow, an evening haul of gnats. Swifts

twist, flick, and beat their wings so fast—one pulse
like two—although wings can't they seem to alternate,
to beat apart. Illusion. To our joy, a make believe.

POSSUM IDYLL

From beyond the patio's light
it stared at me. It became she. Then she
conformed to rules of Tudor portraiture:
pointed chin, black eyes burning,
white-faced little sister to Donne, to our
new, the handsome, Shakespeare. Worried, too—
by the land, the lads, the lazy servants,
her love for the parish sexton holding
the keys. Their velvet burrow, the golden trees.
Oh, how he loves her rat tail, her long lace cuffs
of black, the way each night she sneaks another
morsel in his lap. Carriages await her
but she doesn't care. Her aimless lord
is ruination but forsooth tomorrow
is sufficient. Evil waggles but not
tonight. Venus winks in the sky.

ARIADNE AT SUGARLOAF KEY

Cast out
fishing line tangles in clumps
on the telephone wire,
so many knots of dead bait,
skeletons, lead weights, feathered floats.
Spun nexus of tiny pale fish
and airborne debris. There's

so much in those skeins
of line. Tiny bones and the fish
smell of women, the copper-penny taste of men.
Salt in the air. Wine gods.
One watcher for signs of life
on this abandoned bridge, sidestepping
tide pools of flaking cement and tar.

One speedboat skims under the causeway,
one skiff prods the edge
of mangrove hammock. More
boats reel off into the waters,
a long draw of sparkling wake
out into the ocean,
down the sea stream
among the green islands.

NOTES

The Sappho translation in "For Elizabeth" is by Guy Davenport, *7 Greeks*.

"Theseus Hears the Voice of Ariadne" is the title of a painting by John Sokol.